THE URBAN FOX

The Urban Fox

and other poems

by

Ian Dunlop

for Mary

PAEKAKARIKI PRESS

2016

This is number 201
from an edition of 250 copies.

Text © 2016, Ian Dunlop
Images © 2016, Kirsten Schmidt

Published by Paekakariki Press

ISBN: 978 1 908133 21 2

Typeset in
Monotype Garamond 156
and printed at Paekakariki Press,
Walthamstow

Introduction

Had I the skills of Frost or Larkin, two poets among many I admire, this collection would need no introduction. I hesitate to call them poems. Perhaps they should be called words assembled to look like poems but these words have been carefully chosen to express thoughts and memories which mean something to me. Those who know me well will know what I am referring to, and what I am trying to express. And those who don't I hope will find something which echoes similar experiences and memories in their own lives. It will help, however, if they are getting on in years and have had some experience of London in the 60s. And although some of these themes are sombre most are meant to make my readers smile.

My thanks to Clare Pollard, my tutor at the Poetry School for her advice and her encouragement, to Rob Gordon of iVelocity for his technical help, to Kirsten Schmidt for her illustrations and to Matt McKenzie, a hard but fair taskmaster, for re-introducing me to the wonders of letterpress printing.

IAN DUNLOP

Contents

The Urban Fox

Beneath my window the foxes bark.
Are they in pain or warning
other creatures of the night to stay away?
Or is this eerie screech the sound of mating
by a species determined to survive?

I cannot see them. They lie hidden, not in a copse or wood
across a ploughed field, but
among shrubs and trees
that lie between two blocks of flats
in nondescript Earls Court.

These are urban foxes,
Strong, wily and streetwise.
They roam our patch like hoodies on the prowl,
asserting territorial control,
ready to howl
but not bow before authority.

Returning late at night, I see one padding down the street.
My Ayrshire ancestors would have bristled at the sight.
Brought up to give chase,
they'd have saddled up and followed the hunt
to the fox's hiding place.

Now, outside my mansion block, all I can do
is stand and stare and marvel at
the animal's insolence.
This bushy tailed survivor fears no one.
It looks at me with evident disdain
and slips noiselessly under parked cars,
through garden railings,
to safe hunting and a pain-free night.

Charlotte Street

The Greeks have gone,
the Barbarians are at the gate,
Charlotte Street has changed.
Gone are the cafes where I used to eat
skewers of lamb dusted with oregano,
rice wrapped in vine leaves,
and green pickles that looked like
shrivelled penises.

In sullen post-war London
this was my window to the Adriatic,
to its wine-dark seas and tavernas,
herb and olive oil aromas,
Doric columns bathed in a clear bright light,
and ancient stones once trodden
by the sandalled feet of Plato and his students.

Now the cheap cafes of my youth
have become sleek Asian eateries
where bright young medics
sit at polished wooden tables slurping noodles
soaked in thirty-hour pig broth.

Outside, the street is still a shabby sort of place,
not quite Soho, nor Fitzrovia either.
I study the menus and ask:
'Where are the *koukia* and *kalitsounia* of my youth?'

Pilgrimage

On the road to Compostela
we cross the Pyrenees by the pass of Roncesvalles
where Roland died and
where Charlemagne's retreating army
suffered at the hands of unarmed, rock throwing Basques.

We reach Pamplona
where once in folly I ran before the bulls
falling to the ground and heard
the clatter of hooves on cobbled streets.

Here we rest before taking
the road used by countless pilgrims
in search of salvation from the remains of a dead Saint
buried on the edge of Europe.

We too are pilgrims of a sort,
on an artistic and romantic journey
in search of the stone monuments the others left behind—
those bridges, hospices, abbeys, churches
and that magnificent Cathedral
with its portico to another world.

My memories of that journey are
preserved within the pages of a few travel books on **Spain**,
in some sketches, and a group of faded photos
bound in a dusty album.
They are my proof, if proof is needed,
that I was a pilgrim once
and can wear a coquille on my sleeve.

Juan-les-Pins

Looking at that famous photograph
of Éluard, Penrose and Man Ray,
their topless girl friends, wives and muses,
enjoying a *déjeuner sur l'herbe*
among the woods of the Côte d'Azure,
I remember teenage summers there
yearning for adventure and romance.

The thing about the South of France
is that it is, or was, so goddamn sexy.
The air smelt of pine trees,
thyme, rosemary and wild herbs,
the sea was warm and inviting
and after dark, the crickets
rubbed their legs to start
a symphony of sound,
while moths and other insects of the night
fluttered in the skies in search of light.

Mating
was taking place all around me.
In the backs of cars, in the *cabañas* at Eden Roc,
in grand villas and seedy hotels of the Cap,
in sleek pleasure craft moored in Antibes harbour
and under the upturned hulls of fishing boats.

But in my small teenage world
cloistered with friends and family,
I could see but not touch.
I could yearn but not reach
those adult pleasures just beyond my grasp.

Crocuses

What command prompts you
to poke rude fingers through the ground,
up towards the sky,
at this time of year when the sun
still seems low on the horizon
and we are wrapped in winter coats and scarves?

Has some buried messenger
told you to get ready,
to don your armour of
white, purple and gold,
while the daffodils and narcissi all around you
still huddle in their refuge in the ground.

Or has a sun god issued a command:
'Come on boys, time to get moving!'

You are, after all, the messengers of Spring,
it is your job to tell us the world has turned
and that we are not condemned for ever
to the cold grey skies of winter.

Soon the almond trees will blossom
and waxy magnolias will let
their creamy white flowers reveal
their hidden beauty.

Soon blue will be seen in the skies.
Nothing, not even man,
can stop the sun from rising,
nor crocuses from raising
our hopes again.

Maybe

When I walked the Wicklow Hills
an Irish mist obscured the view,
my eyes lay on the stony road ahead
cut through peat bog and past lumps of rotting heather.
We were a band of students escaping the smoke-filled pubs
of this far from fair, fair city.

We joked and laughed but my attention lay elsewhere,
on a long-limbed sad-eyed beauty with a nervous laugh
and a beguiling smile.
We first met at a Dublin party,
and sat beside each other on a staircase
of a Georgian town house in terminal decay.

'Can we meet again?' I asked,
'Maybe' she said.

And so here we were a few days later
walking the Wicklow Hills
wondering what would happen.

Our romance began with many meetings, many partings,
moments of great joy and great pain,
of betrayals, rival lovers, and nights walking
the Dublin Canal in despair.
And always letters,
hers in a round hand, mine in an italic script,
a few never thrown away.

One moment survives those confusing days.
A meeting in fog-bound Edinburgh,
so thick you had to feel your way along the railings
    of the street
to a guest house which required shillings in the meter.

Then she did say 'yes'.

But 'yes' is not a word she uses often.
Even now, sixty years later, she likes to keep me guessing.
'Would you like to see a movie?' I ask.
'Maybe', she says.

On the Road from San Giovanni

We met in the Brancacci chapel
where we gazed up
at the frescos by Masaccio
and wondered why Adam shields his eyes
and not his nakedness.

On a whim my painter friend and I
decided to leave a bottle of chianti
on the doorstep of the house in San Giovanni
where Tommaso was born.

It was a libation to a god of painting
who died at twenty six
before becoming famous
but would in time impress
Michelangelo no less.

And then on the road back to Florence,
a flash of anger, a sudden change of mood.
It was soon apparent my new friend,
who had abandoned wife and family for his art,
was no gentle Florentine
but a Caravaggio in Rome.

Then and there I realised
that to become an artist soldier
requires a painful sacrifice.
Even Adam had Eve beside him
on the road from Paradise.

The Duke in Kilburn

'De, de, da de' blew Louis at the start of West End Blues.
'Dang, ding, dang, ding dang' banged the Duke on his
    piano,
before taking his band on the A-train down from Harlem.
'I can't get no ...' shouted Mick, in his strange Athenian
    costume,
in mock frustration at his lack of action.

Why do these riffs and chords
still rattle round my brain
sixty years after they were first heard
on slick black discs
bought from Dobell's on St Martin's Lane?

Why, when so much else has been forgotten,
do I still remember when
two friends and I
persuaded the Headmaster of a very ancient school
to grant permission to attend
the Duke and his orchestra
in a far off cinema in Kilburn?

Or that moment in LA
when, for the first time, I truly was far away from home
and heard Dylan sing
and watched the audience bring out their zippos
and light flames to life on the road alone.

Or years later, at Shea,
when the Stones renewed
the rock anthems of my youth.
We in the bleachers and the upper stands
of this famous baseball stadium
sang with them and
somewhere in the middle a wall of sound was formed
which must have made the angels dance in heaven.

The Return

After many days of cloud and rain
I head north and have never seen
England look more beautiful.
From the windows of the train
I gaze at fields of glistening water,
and hills with pregnant sheep.
We pass cooling towers belching steam,
market cities, working farms and a lone church
abandoned by its parishioners standing
in a bright green field.

We stop at York and glimpse the Minster,
past Durham and its citadel cathedral.
And then I see the outstretched wings of the Angel of the
    North
welcoming travellers to the border lands across the Tyne
    and Tweed.

On to Scotland
where my trader forebears lived and worked,
where I was born and where I spent
happy days playing golf and looking out to sea,
but, as the great Doctor predicted,
I kept an eye out for the high road
which would take me back to England.

Details

Was it her smooth white bottom
which first turned me on?
Or the little black triangle between her legs
which I noticed when we swam
in a waterfall below
Mont Saint-Victoire?

Is it the details in a painting
which catch and enchant the eye?
The dabs of paint by the Provençal master
which slowly come together to form
a card player or an apple.

Or Vermeer's little patch of yellow
which links the houses on a Dutch canal
and which Proust remembered
lying sleepless in his cork-lined room.

Or those discarded wooden slippers
in the Arnolfini portrait, a hint of disorder
in the lives of a well-dressed couple
standing in a very tidy room.

Does the devil use these details,
to catch the unwary passer-by?
Does he lie in wait, and, like a lizard,
flick out a tongue to snatch a fly?

It is the details which obsess us,
the little things we do not see,
the hooks that bind a bra-strap,
the zips and buttons that lie hidden,
waiting for fumbling fingers to set free.

Berkeley Square

There like a beached whale,
lay the giant plane,
brought down the night before
by a hurricane
not meant to happen.

Even this great warrior,
with all its ancient armour
of roots and limbs,
could not withstand
a late November storm.

How are the mighty fallen!
I said as I slunk to my place of work
across the Square.
Soon the woodcutters will arrive
and sever the branches
from your mighty silver torso.

Soon there will be no trace of you
except a tree stump in the ground.
And what will happen to that elusive bird
which found refuge in your branches
and sang to the night people prowling down below?

When Where

When the snow forms white lines along the boughs,
when the sky remains an impassive grey,
when the streets are scuffed with muddy feet,
when the sun stays hidden and sulks all day,
you know the time has come to dream

of India instead

where the statues are garlanded in bright orange flowers,
where the elephants are caparisoned in purple and gold,
where the men wear turbans of saffron and red,
where the women wear saris of colourful thread,
and the waves leave white lines of foam in the sand.

My Sleeping Beauty

My Sleeping Beauty
may have grey hair and look prematurely old
but to me she is still beautiful
as she slumbers by the kitchen table,
her head resting on a pillow,
her eyes closed and a faint smile on her lips.

No Prince Charming
can wake her now from wordless dreams.
No kiss can kindle a spark of recognition.
Nothing now can bring her back to the world
she once ruled with sharp eye
and an untamed tongue.

She is lost in a universe of her own making,
shuffling cards, creating a kaleidoscope of
Jacks, Kings, Queens, Aces—
Spades, Clubs, Diamonds, Hearts.
Sometimes if you say her name
she looks up to see who's talking,
before returning to her dreams.
'She is lost to the world', friends say.
But, while she still breathes and smiles
she is not lost to me.

She remains my Alice in Wonderland.
My Sleeping Beauty.

Lost Sapphire

The thief came in the night
while my mother slept
not to rob her of her life,
(another would do that),
but to remove the jewels
that were her history.

These she wore like medals
for valour sustained in love's wars,
symbols of past conquests, and
tributes to her beauty.

In later life she never ventured out
without a brooch on her lapel
and pearls round her neck.
And when we admired them she would say:
'These will be yours one day.'

But there she lay,
stick thin and close to dying,
falling in and out of sleep,
while someone came and found
the keys to her safe
and her hopes of immortality.

We never knew who took them
or for what purpose.
We suspect they went to help
a carer get through
their own battle with failing health.

We never told our mum.
And so she died
still thinking the pale blue sapphire,
(destined for my wife)
would remain with us for ever
and remind us of her life.

Dilemmas

'Lánguidos muchachitos',
they called us in the local paper,
as we lazed round a pool in Southern Spain.
Three etiolated former public schoolboys,
building up a tan,
reading our Durrell and our Brenan,
hoping to find our own Justine
among the Andalusian clan.

No roll of drums, no trumpet blast
announced their arrival but our hosts appeared from
    nowhere
bringing with them a matador, a modern Escamillo,
fresh from the bull ring
where he had been showered with trophies
cut from a beast he had just slaughtered—
ears, hooves and even a tail.

He was film-star handsome,
olive skin, black hair,
a broad smile and a killer's eyes.
Round him gathered his quadrille,
and bullfight aficionados.

Suddenly, among the throng I saw
a famous author, the one I most admired
in the world I was just beginning to discover.
With his grey hair and beard, broad chest,
face burnt by the sun and
battles with men, women, booze,

the wild animals of Africa
and big fish in the sea—
he was my Socrates.

His hand now shook, his eyes looked red,
he had no doubt been drinking the rosé
he kept in a hold-all by his side.
But he still liked to keep in shape,
swimming twenty lengths a day,
his head out of the water,
a grey-haired otter in a trout pool.
And, like Hercules, he often carried
a massive wooden club
to keep his wrists supple and his fingers from seizing up.

'Hombre, hombre!' which one would you
choose to follow:
the man at ease in his skin,
the athlete with a ballet dancer's legs,
a cool head, quick reflexes, and a steady hand;
or the great writer, a body in decline and
a mind riddled with self doubt?
The man with the sword
or the one with the pen?

Before I could find an answer
another dilemma came:
A call from home announced the death
of my Scottish grandfather.
Should I return for the funeral of a man I hardly knew,
or should I stay and drink in every word and action
of this glamorous adult world I now had access to?

In the end I don't think I decided
but was pushed on to a 'plane
back to the cold grey North
and away from the temptations of the South.

In life, we often face hard choices—
which path to take in the woods,
which girl to ask to dance and which to marry,
which job to accept and which to refuse.

My advice, for what it's worth, is not to choose.
Let the gods decide, let someone else take charge.
Let the wind take the leaf wherever it may land
and you will never have to worry
whether you made the right choice in the end.

The Tall Man at Muirfield

Every Saturday the tall man comes to Muirfield.
He stands erect, his pale blue eyes look out to sea.
He's lost his wife and recently his Alsatian
and bears the scars of reaching eighty three.

He still carries clubs, walks eighteen holes,
and speaks with the dignified tones
of an Edinburgh professional man
who now finds he is on his own.

Today he wonders whether the time has come
to give up golf. He takes some practice swings,
fluffs a chip, hooks a drive and says:
'This could be my final fling.'

But some atavistic urge tells him to keep going
'While there is golf there's life', I hear him say,
He picks up his bag and walks on through the rough:
'Now is not the time to throw my clubs away.'

Please God

Please God, stop the leaves from falling,
tell the trees to keep their great achievement,
ask the winds to hold their breath
and command the rain clouds: 'stay away'.
Soon the winds will shake these branches
sending leaves down to the grey wet pavement
to be gathered by our local Lithuanian,
bagged and taken ignominiously away.

Please God, I ask the same for Mary.
Tell the moon not to rise this evening,
ask the earth to refrain from turning
and keep the sun from sinking
into the dark foreboding sea.
Let's keep Mary as she is—
smiling, wordless, but content—
lost to the daily world but still dreaming
of time past and better days ahead.

'I can't stop time', I hear you say.
But is it heresy to ask:

'With my camera in Hyde Park this morning,
the sun was out and the leaves flickered in the breeze.
The shutter clicked—time froze for one glorious moment.
So if I can stop time
why cannot you?'

Look Forth

My idea of heaven is a patch of high ground
looking out to sea across the Firth of Forth
to the Paps of Fife and the fishing villages of East Neuk.
Turn round, and over fields of corn and barley,
you can see the purple hills that are the Lammermuirs.
And to the West, past Gullane Hill,
the distinctive outline of King Arthur's Seat
stretched across the sky like a bumpy armchair.

Don't stand too long.
A wind from the North can bring an arctic chill
and rain can sweep in from nowhere.
Soon this little corner will turn to hell
and, like King Lear, you will howl with pain.
There is no shelter here, but when I die,
scatter my ashes near this spot
and I can find some rest between heaven and hell.

Eleven Eleven

There is no memorial to you, my friends.
You escaped the war but died in other battles.
You had your fights with cancer,
weak hearts and with Aids.
One was murdered in a jealous rage
by a hitchhiker on a Route Nationale in France.

Where are you now, my friends?
In heaven? I think not.
That's why it is so important
for us, the survivors in life's trenches,
to remember your names and say:
'He was a friend of mine.'

Tim, John, Nichol, David,
George, Sidney, Hugh.

But when my memory goes, what next?
What will happen when even your descendants
are not here to mourn?
Take heart, one day we will all join the big unknown,
the world that existed before the big bang,
where gravestones, even words, are not needed.

Too Late

Is it too late for love,
is it too late to dance,
is it too late to make a move
across the floor and glance
at a pretty face
otherwise engaged
and wonder whether
you stand a chance?

Surely you are too old
for such licentious thoughts.
You may think you can be bold
but really you ought
to be more careful.

There was a time of course
when you had no thoughts at all.
You blithely went through life
not thinking of a fall.

But now things have changed,
you have to be responsible.
And love has perhaps become
no longer possible.